JBIO
JOAN

ROBERTS, JEREMY
SAINT JOAN OF ARC

Saint JOAN OF ARC

Jeremy Roberts

Lerner Publications Company
Minneapolis

Lerner Publications Company
A division of Lerner Publishing Group
241 First Avenue North
Minneapolis, MN 55401 U.S.A.

Website address: www.lernerbooks.com

Library of Congress Cataloging-in-Publication Data

Roberts, Jeremy, 1956–
    Saint Joan of Arc / by Jeremy Roberts.
      p. cm. — (A&E biography)
    Includes bibliographical references and index.
    Summary: A biography of the young French woman who, inspired by visions supposedly from God, led the French army against English invaders, was burned at the stake as a heretic, and eventually was declared a saint.
    ISBN 0-8225-4981-6 (lib. bdg. : alk. paper)
    1. Joan, of Arc, Saint 1412–1431—Juvenile literature. 2. Christian women saints—France—Biography—Juvenile literature. 3. Hundred Years' War, 1339–1453—Juvenile literature. 4. France—History—Charles VII, 1422–1461—Juvenile literature. [1. Joan, of Arc, Saint, 1412–1431. 2. Saints. 3. Women Biography.] I. Title. II. Series.
DC103.5.R63 2000
944'.026'092-dc21
    [B]   99-33498

Manufactured in the United States of America
1 2 3 4 5 6 – JR – 05 04 03 02 01 00

CONTENTS

Jehanette said she began to hear the voices of saints and angels when she was thirteen years old.

Chapter **ONE**

THE VOICES

THE VOICES CAME TO HER IN THE PASTURE, speaking to her as she watched her father's animals. Jehanette was used to them, or at least as used to them as anyone could be. They were awesome, the wildest thing that had ever happened in her small village. But they were frightening as well. For she knew they came from God.

The voices came with a bright light. They were the voices of saints and angels. No one else could hear them or see the light. They had been coming for several years, since Jehanette was thirteen years old. Usually Jehanette heard them when she was near the church, the center of village life. She knew better than to tell anyone about them.

The voices had always given her a simple direction: Be a good girl. Others in the small village of Domrémy, in what is now France, say she succeeded very well. Jehanette was known as one of Domrémy's most devout girls. She went to church often. She obeyed the Ten Commandments and her parents. She took care of the sick. She was a virgin and tried to be a perfect Catholic.

The voices helped her do all of this. But this day, they told her to do a bold, impossible thing: She must leave her home and save France and the king.

Jehanette began to cry. In the light that accompanied the voices, a shape appeared. Gradually it formed into an angel, the most powerful of the army that fought Satan—the archangel Michael. He spoke softly, telling Jehanette not to be afraid. Her country and her king were in great need, and God wanted her to help them.

The year was 1429, and though Jehanette was just a teenager in a tiny town far from the big cities of the time, she did not need an angel to tell her that things were bad in France. The country had been wracked by war for nearly one hundred years. The countryside across the river from her village was controlled by the king's enemies. In fact, the king had not even been officially crowned. His father had gone insane, and many said that the king himself was weak.

As if war wasn't bad enough, for the past eighty years France had been devastated by the Black Plague. There was no cure for this epidemic disease.

The house where Jehanette was born and the church where she was baptized in Domrémy, Lorraine (modern-day France)

First striking in 1348, the plague wiped out between one-third and one-half of France's population. At first the deaths were so overwhelming that bodies were piled and left to rot in the streets. After the first outbreaks, the disease came back in waves in different places. It was impossible to know where or if it would break out again.

It was during this time of distress and uncertainty that the archangel Michael insisted that Jehanette leave the simple one-story houses and open pastures of her village and the surrounding countryside.

Jehanette reported that the archangel Michael appeared to her many times while she lived in Domrémy.

Before, she had always obeyed the voices, but this time she hesitated. Many dangers lurked in the war-torn countryside. Anyone—especially a poor peasant girl—could easily be robbed, or much worse. It wasn't fear that delayed Jehanette, though. She knew her parents would worry about her if she left, and she did not want to hurt them.

But Michael and the voices of the saints could not be ignored. When the voices stopped and the light faded, Jehanette decided to find a way to obey.

A WITCH AND A SAINT

In the years since that fateful vision, the fame of that village girl has spread far beyond Domrémy. For Jehanette, also called Jeanne, is known to us as Saint Joan of Arc.

Different theories have been put forth about the voices she said she heard. Many modern people do not believe that an angel appeared and spoke to her. Some people suggest that she had hallucinations or that she suffered from a mental illness. Some believe that she simply made up the story of the voices.

Whatever the explanation, Joan of Arc acted as if the voices were real. And they launched her on an incredible journey to help the king and to reunite France. Before the year was out, she would be called both a witch and a saint.

She would also help change France—and the world.

Joan of Arc as a little girl

Chapter **TWO**

A PEASANT GIRL

THE FRANCE WHERE JOAN HEARD THE ARCHANGEL
Michael speak to her was a very different place than
the modern European country. In fifteenth-century
France, there were no factories. The lives of most people,
especially countryfolk like Joan's family, revolved around
the church and farming. Country people made their own
clothes, raised sheep and other livestock, and spent
much of their free time in church-related activities. Both
men and women had well-defined roles in society.

The differences were also political. The land was divided into many small kingdoms, known as fiefs. According to the laws of the times, the head of each fief
owed allegiance to the king. But military and
financial power often overshadowed the law.

Many fiefs on French soil were under control of the English king. He was related to ancient French kings and claimed to be the rightful king of France. The heads of some fiefs were so powerful that they could ignore both the French and the English king, or ally themselves with whichever king they chose. The most powerful of these leaders owned a fief called Burgundy. He was the Duke of Burgundy, and he was allied with England.

The conflict between the English and French kings dated back to 1337. Called the Hundred Years' War, the conflict actually continued, on and off, longer than that. It was fought for riches and for control of different parts of France, as well as for the right to be king of all of France. The long war saw a great many brutal battles, with civilians killed as well as soldiers. Cities that were loyal to the enemy were often looted and sometimes destroyed.

In the thirteenth century, before the war, France was one of the richest places in Europe, home to great universities and cathedrals. But the disasters of war and plague in the fourteenth century changed everything. People found it difficult to survive, let alone prosper. The economy was wrecked.

Charles V, king of France from 1364 to 1380, managed to recover many of the lands that France had lost to England. Although he was very popular with the French people, the country still had problems. War with England continued. Charles's death in 1380

In Joan's time, most common people worked in agriculture.

once again plunged France into dark times.

His son, Charles VI, suffered a mental breakdown in 1392. After that, the English and the princes of the small fiefdoms divided up France. One historian labels the period from 1400 to 1428 with one word: anarchy. France was like a beautiful painting cut into tiny pieces and jumbled up into a mess.

In 1420, Charles VI signed a treaty that turned the kingdom over to the English. The treaty disinherited his son, Charles, the Dauphin, meaning that he would never be king. (*Dauphin* is a French word that refers to the first son and heir of the king.) The treaty also said that the English would control France forever.

The English already occupied much of northern France. They had an alliance with the powerful Duke of Burgundy, who ruled a large area of the countryside. When Charles VI died in 1422, Henry VI of England— only ten months old—was declared king of France.

The Dauphin fled to a castle in the Loire Valley. He opposed the English—and his father's surrender to them. The Dauphin called himself king and had some allies. But he was only nineteen years old, and his forces were not very powerful. Much of his army was massacred in a fight at Verneuil in 1424. Afterward, he was deeply discouraged, doubting his ability and right to be king.

Young King Henry VI was declared king of France when he was only ten months old.

It was into this chaos that Joan of Arc was born. Her town, Domrémy, was in eastern France, near modern-day Switzerland and the main road to Germany. It was located on the march, or border, of two sections of France: Lorraine and Champagne. The land was hilly and fertile, bisected by rivers and streams. Considered part of Lorraine, Domrémy was far from the major cities and centers of power.

The Duke of Lorraine was loyal to the Dauphin. But immediately across the river from Domrémy was a town called Maxey, which was allied with Burgundy. The two villages often fought. At times, the people of Domrémy took their animals to a safe place in the local hills, fearing attacks by the Burgundian forces.

THE SAINTS

There are no exact records, but Joan was probably born in 1412, the daughter of a peasant farmer, Jacques Darc (or d'Arc), and Isabelle Romée. The family was not rich, but by the standards of the time, they were not poor either. Besides farming and raising animals, Jacques held an important job helping to collect taxes in the town. Most biographers believe that Joan had three brothers and one sister, but historians hold different opinions as to their birth order.

Society in those days was strictly divided by class. Roles were rigid. At the top of society was the king, then the great dukes and nobles. Peasants were far, far below them. A man who was born a peasant would usually stay a peasant until he died. His children and grandchildren would also be peasants. In most cases, peasants were powerless against the dukes and nobles. They owed their allegiance to the local lord and had to obey him. Democracy was unheard of.

A girl born into this society was expected to follow her father's wishes. In general, peasant girls married other peasants who lived nearby. They were expected to obey their husbands and raise a family. Rarely did any peasant, especially a girl, challenge authority or society's rules.

Until Joan was thirteen, there was little about her that set her apart from the other girls in her village. Like most country girls, she was not taught to read or write. Like them, she learned to sew and spin. She also watched the family animals from time to time. Others in the village thought she was very religious. Years later, many remembered her good works as a young girl.

Joan's first experience with the mysterious voices came around noon during a summer's day. She was in her father's garden. The voices came from her right—from the direction of the church. That, she said later, was how she first knew they must have come from God and not the devil.

Joan was afraid, but the voices calmed her. Their message was reassuring: Be a good girl. Obey the commandments. Go to church. Remain a virgin.

Besides the archangel Michael, Joan said that Saints Catherine and Margaret had spoken to her. The saints' voices were always sweet and mild and were often accompanied by their images. When they were, Joan could see halos around their heads and crowns of jewels.

Joan obeyed the voices, going to church often and doing other good acts. Joan lived in a time when religion was extremely important for everyone. Nearly everyone in France was Catholic. The church was a major part of everyday life. Joan had several godmothers and godfathers and knew the parish priest very well.

Though the people of Joan's time believed it was unusual for angels and saints to appear, they still thought it could happen. Many religious men and women, like Joan, believed that God, the saints, or angels spoke directly to them.

The voices that spoke to Joan continued for about five years, in different places and times. One day, they told Joan that she must help the Dauphin and save France. Joan was torn by this message. She knew that her father and mother did not want her to leave the village.

She said later that her father had had dreams that she would leave with the army. He had told her brothers that he wouldn't let that happen—women who followed the army in those days were considered prostitutes. Joan's father said that her brothers should drown her if she left—and if they didn't, he would.

Joan did not tell her parents what the voices had told her. But through the dreams, or some other way, her father and mother seemed to sense her plans. They did everything they could to prevent her from leaving the small village. They wanted her to marry a young man who claimed she had promised to marry him. But Joan refused. The young man even took her to court for breaking her promise. But Joan was able to convince the judges that she had never agreed to marry him. She was intent on keeping her virginity, as she had promised the voices.

Still, she did not do all they asked. Two or three times a week, the angels came and told her she must leave for the good of France. Their command became even more specific—she must free the city of Orléans, which had been surrounded by the English army.

Joan argued, telling the angels that she was only a girl who knew nothing of war. She did not even know how to ride a horse correctly. But the archangel Michael assured her she would succeed. The voices said she must go to a town called Vaucouleurs, more than ten miles to the north of Domrémy. There, she would find a captain named Robert de Baudricourt, who would have her taken to the Dauphin and Orléans.

To resist her father, to travel through a countryside wracked by war—those things were difficult. To free a city surrounded by an entire army, to help crown a king—those were incredible.

The angels appear to Joan.

But Joan firmly believed that the angels were real and had been sent by God. And she knew she must find a way to obey them.

"I was obedient in everything," she later recalled, speaking about her parents, who wanted her to settle down near them. "But since God had commanded it, I must do it. And since God had commanded it, had I had a hundred fathers and a hundred mothers, and had I been a king's daughter, I would have gone."

When Joan appeared before Robert de Baudricourt and asked him to take her to the Dauphin, he scoffed at her.

Chapter **THREE**

IN A MAN'S CLOTHES

ROBERT DE BAUDRICOURT, THE CAPTAIN OF Vaucouleurs, was amazed. Before him stood a simple country girl, her long hair pulled back and tied in the common style, her worn red dress modestly falling to the ground. She seemed unremarkable in every way but one: She wanted the captain to arrange to take her to the Dauphin. She claimed God himself had spoken to her, telling her that she had to help the Dauphin, that he had to be crowned king, and that Joan was to help him reunite the kingdom of France under his rule.

The girl was a simple peasant, no different from any other girl in this fortified town far from the heart of France. She was supposed to be getting married and having children, not talking wildly of angels and adventures. And yet, even as he scoffed at her during that cold winter of 1429, he realized that there was something special about the girl, this Joan of Arc.

She had tried against all odds to do what the voices had told her to do. She had sneaked away from her parents' house, pretending that she was going to visit her uncle and aunt to help them care for a newborn baby. More important, she had managed to convince others that the voices were real and should be obeyed. And many of those she convinced were sober and logical men, including her uncle, who had brought her to de Baudricourt.

When de Baudricourt was first approached by Joan's uncle, his reaction had been simple: He told the uncle to take the girl back to her father. But now, with Joan before him and with others testifying about her beliefs, de Baudricourt was not so sure what to do.

The captain—like nearly everyone else in this era—believed that if Joan were truly hearing voices, there were only two possibilities about their source. One was God and the angels, as Joan claimed. The other was the devil.

Several days before, de Baudricourt and the parish priest had gone to the house in Vaucouleurs where Joan was staying. The priest began praying, trying to cast out any demons that might possess her. Joan only smiled and welcomed him, showing that she was not possessed by the devil.

Joan seeks advice about the heavenly voices that ordered her to help Charles VII become king of France.

What's more, a legend had made the rounds some time before about a maid—a virgin—from the Lorraine area who would save France. It was the sort of vague rumor that floated around from time to time among gossips. But this girl *was* a maid, this *was* Lorraine, and some people wondered if perhaps the prediction was about to come true.

The country had been at war for so very long. Could de Baudricourt afford to dismiss someone who might be able to help France just because she was a girl and a peasant? He had delayed as long as he could. Finally, he decided to let her go to the Dauphin.

A DANGEROUS JOURNEY

Historians speculate that Robert de Baudricourt sent a message to the Dauphin's court to ask for advice before making his final decision. The Dauphin was staying in the Loire Valley, in a castle called Chinon. It was 250 miles away as the crow flew—and much farther by road. Even by horse, the journey over the poor roads of the time would take many days. The enemy controlled much of the land in between.

Two soldiers were chosen to accompany Joan on her journey, along with four servants. Because she would be traveling through enemy territory, she was given male clothing to wear as a disguise. Her hair was cut like a boy's. The captain also gave her a sword before sending her on her way.

The roads were filled with enemy soldiers. But the enemy was not all Joan had to fear—for the two men accompanying her decided along the way to try to rape her. At the very least, they thought they could talk her into having sex with them. But as the men were about to attack Joan, something mysterious happened. One man later said that as he approached her, he was overcome with great shame. He felt from that

The earliest-known image of Joan of Arc is shown in this French detail from the Parliament Council register at Domrémy.

point on that Joan was truly on a mission from God and that it would be a great sin to do anything to hurt that mission.

Some historians believe that dressing in men's clothes may have helped Joan keep her virginity. While dresses of the era usually reached to the ground, women and girls did not wear underpants, and their clothes provided little protection. On the other hand, men's hose fully covered the legs and hips. Joan kept her clothes on "tied and tight" when she slept, one of the men later said.

Many of the specifics about Joan's life are unknown, and it is impossible to say for certain whether the clothes helped keep her safe from rape. It's possible that she fought off one or both of the men or talked them out of attacking her. It's even possible that they made up the story and never tried to do anything to her. In any event, it appears that both men came to believe in Joan's voices during the journey.

For eleven days, Joan and her companions traveled the difficult roads, fording streams and rivers, which were starting to flood with the spring thaw. To avoid enemy soldiers, they often traveled at night. Attending Mass was extremely important to devout Catholics; Joan had always done so as often as she could in Domrémy. It grieved her that she could not attend Mass in the towns they passed, but the men said that stopping in town would be too dangerous.

As the group traveled southwest, they began to parallel the Loire River. Castles and cities, surrounded by massive walls and stone towers, threw dark shadows across their path. These thick fortresses were a contradiction. Once inside the walls of a castle or city, a person could be safe—or trapped. If the city were surrounded by the enemy, as Orléans was, people inside might be cut off from supplies of food and water. Hope could slip away over a period of weeks, leaving only surrender—or starvation and death.

Joan was undaunted; she urged her companions on. They passed Orléans, cut off from them by the river and the English. They continued west to Chinon and the Dauphin. By now, rumors that Joan was coming had spread. Already she had enemies among the

Dauphin's advisers, who feared she might be trying to trick them.

The Dauphin's forces were weak and had recently suffered a great loss in battle, but that did not deter Joan. Nothing would stop her from her mission. She knew she would soon free the besieged city of Orléans and help crown the Dauphin king.

Joan of Arc entering Orléans

Chapter **FOUR**

TAKE ME TO ORLÉANS

ALL WAS DESPAIR. THE DAUPHIN'S HOPES TO BE king, to reunite the kingdom, to expel the English and rule France—these were lofty dreams that mocked him now. His armies could not win even a small skirmish. Much of his land was occupied by the enemy. Even the city of Orléans, once a stronghold, was surrounded by English soldiers.

To Charles the Dauphin, son of the mad king, the winter of 1429 was a desperate time. The Dauphin's confidence was gone. If he had been bold once, he was now only depressed. Chinon, his sprawling castle overlooking the Vienne River, was as much a prison as a fortress. Its walls were hung with rich tapestries. Its white and yellow stones faced the Loire River. Its

large hall and apartments hosted many pleasant en-
tertainments. But the thick, damp air of winter per-
meated the grounds and the Dauphin's mood.

Word had reached him of a peasant girl from Lorraine coming because voices told her that he was the
true king. His advisers were divided about this girl,
Joan of Arc. Some feared that she was part of a plot
by forces allied with the Dauphin's wife and her
mother. They were trying to use the simple girl and
her "voices" to gain power, the advisers thought.

To the Dauphin, the rumors were fantastical—difficult to believe. Supposedly, the voices had told the
peasant girl that she would lead the army in war. This
was unthinkable. A girl in a war? A peasant lead an
army? Crazy notions.

Perhaps, had his troops been winning many battles,
the Dauphin would not have bothered with the peasant girl. Perhaps, had he felt surer of himself, he
would not have listened to someone who claimed to
have a message from God. Or perhaps her devotion
and faith would have convinced him no matter what
the circumstances. In any event, he consented to allow
her to see him in the castle.

Not convinced that Joan was for real, the Dauphin
gathered more than three hundred knights around
him in the great hall of Chinon. He mingled with
them in the torchlight, almost hiding himself, dis-
guised as one of them. But Joan went straight to him.

"I'm not the king," he told her.

But she threw herself to the floor. Holding his knees, she told him that she knew he was the Dauphin. "My name is Joan the Maid," she said in her soft voice. "The King of Heaven brings you word through me that you shall be anointed and crowned in the city of Reims and that you shall be the lieutenant of the Heavenly King, Who is the King of France."

FRANCE'S TRUE HEIR

Those who witnessed the scene said that the Dauphin seemed transformed by Joan. He took her away from the others and listened as she again told him he was the son of the king and was France's true heir. The

At first, the Dauphin didn't believe the rumors surrounding Joan and her mission.

people in the hall marveled at Joan, impressed by the boldness of a mere teenager. But she did not convince everyone, and even the Dauphin wanted more proof that what she claimed was true—or at least not an elaborate plot to trick him.

He had her questioned by experts in religion and other fields. Their examination took more than a month. Again and again, Joan repeated the story of the voices. The examiners challenged her: If God wishes to deliver the people of France, he doesn't need an army, said one. Joan answered that it would be by the will of God that the army would save France.

The examiners debated for some time, asking for a sign that what she said was true. They wanted a miracle. Joan told them that she had not come there to show a sign. "But take me to Orléans, and I will show you the signs for which I have been sent," she told them.

In the meantime, men were sent back to Domrémy to look into Joan's background. They learned that she had been a devout and—until the voices told her to leave—obedient girl.

If the people of the Middle Ages believed in God, they also believed in the devil. And, to their minds, there was always the possibility that the devil, not God, was speaking to Joan. She could be possessed—under the devil's control. She could even be a witch, working with the devil on purpose.

While people believed that the devil had great pow-

Joan was questioned by numerous experts to determine if she was telling the truth about her mission. After the examinations, few people doubted her.

ers, there were some things, according to the beliefs of the time, that he could not do. For one thing, he could not possess a virgin. Joan had always claimed to be a virgin. If she was, then she could not have been sent by the devil. If she had lied about this claim, possessed or not, then why believe her about anything else?

And so Joan's ultimate test became her chastity. The Dauphin's mother-in-law examined the girl, finding that she had told the truth. "In her is found no evil," declared the examiners finally. "But only good, humility, virginity, devotion, honesty, simplicity."

A CERTAIN ELEGANCE

The camera had not been invented, and there are no lifelike paintings of Joan from her time. A letter written by one of the king's advisers several months after the meeting at Chinon describes her as having a "virile bearing"—active and energetic as well as strong. She was clearly not a timid or meek young woman, for otherwise she could not have come so far. In fact, she must have been very strong, not only to fight but also to wear armor for days and nights on end—as the future would soon prove.

"This Maid has a certain elegance," said the adviser, Perceval de Boulainvilliers. He said that Joan didn't talk much, but that she used her words well and wisely. "She has a pretty, woman's voice, eats little, drinks very little wine," he told a friend. "She enjoys riding a horse and takes pleasure in fine arms, greatly likes the company of noble fighting men, detests numerous assemblies and meetings, readily sheds copious tears, has a cheerful face."

Above all, Joan was chaste and devoted to God, seeking to go to Mass, make confession, and receive Communion. She was called a maid; in French the word is *pucelle*, and it means "virgin." Devout Catholics believe that Jesus' mother, Mary, was a virgin when he was conceived by God. There was no better model of devotion and perfect behavior than the Virgin Mary.

LAST CHANCE FOR ORLÉANS?

The city of Orléans was in horrible shape. The Dauphin was desperate. Joan claimed that if she were given soldiers, she could free the city.

The Dauphin's examiners said there was no reason

to doubt her. They assured him that it was not unlawful to let her lead the army. His own mother-in-law had vouched for Joan's truthfulness and purity. Many advisers who had started out skeptical now believed that God was speaking to her.

But it was still the Dauphin's decision. Something about the young girl had touched him—something

Joan was a devout Catholic who desired to go to Mass, make confession, and receive Communion.

more than just her words that she would see him crowned at Reims, the ancient capital of France. Some historians think the Dauphin worried that he was an illegitimate child—and therefore not the true heir to the throne. Joan said she had a message from God that she could tell only the Dauphin. Many historians think she assured him that he was not illegitimate and that he was rightfully king.

Some historians believe that the Dauphin was in such desperate shape that he decided he had nothing to lose by listening to Joan. Whatever the reason, he gave Joan of Arc a sizable force to command. He also had a suit of armor—white or unmarked—made for her, and he gave her a black horse.

Gathering her army in the nearby city of Tours, Joan ordered that a standard, or flag, be made, so that her troops could follow it into battle. On the flag's blue background, Jesus Christ sat on a cloud, blessing the fleur-de-lis, the emblem of the king of France, held by an angel. A few days later, Joan had a banner made. It showed the crucifixion of Jesus.

She gathered the army's priests and soldiers around the banner, where they sang hymns to Jesus' mother, Mary. Joan expected all the soldiers to confess their sins and demanded the best behavior from them, even telling them not to curse. They seemed to believe in her vision so much that they obeyed, at least when she was nearby. Joan knew at least one of the soldiers very well—her brother Pierre had come from Dom-

Joan of Arc leading her army

rémy to join her. (Some historians think her brother Jean also fought by her side.)

Joan had all the equipment that a captain of an army should have—armor, a horse, and assistants. And as she prepared to march into battle, the voices provided a weapon. They told her a sword would be found near the altar of a country church, Sainte-Catherine de Fierbois. At the church, her men discovered a rusted sword, buried with several crosses.

Wearing the sword her standard waving above her, Joan led her army toward Orléans, about one hundred miles away.

Fearless and guided by God, Joan of Arc and her soldiers battled the English at Orléans.

Chapter **FIVE**

VICTORY

ORLÉANS, **LOCATED ON THE NORTHERN BANK OF** the Loire River, had been surrounded by an English army since the fall of 1428. The English controlled the river's northern bank, as well as a bridge that connected the city with the southern bank. They also controlled the river west of the city, cutting off help from that direction.

There were two ways to defeat an enemy walled in behind a castle or fortified city during the Middle Ages. The first was to battle against the doorways and walls, breaking them down and taking the defenses head-on. A strong army striking quickly could then overrun the defenders. But this method could result in a lot of casualties, and possibly defeat, for the attackers.

The second way took much longer—but it was easier. The attackers surrounded the enemy's stronghold, cutting it off from the rest of the countryside. They then launched stones and arrows from cannons, catapults, and large crossbows. They might also set parts of the castle or town on fire, undermine its walls, or even poison its water supply.

But, most of all, the attackers waited. Their best weapon was hunger—the hunger of the people in the city or castle that was surrounded. Sooner or later, the defenders would run out of food. When that happened, they would surrender or die—or perhaps both.

It was not just the army that was attacked. Everyone in the city or castle—women and children included—could be killed once a siege began. All were considered the enemy.

The French trapped in the city of Orléans made several attempts to break the siege, but the English were too strong. The French forces outside could not coordinate themselves for a mass attack. A raid on the English in February 1429 ended in disaster. As the winter wore on, the situation became bleaker and bleaker. Some Frenchmen were able to sneak food into the city, but not much. Only one gate remained open, and the road near it was controlled by an English fort.

Even though the English forces had the upper hand, the situation outside Orléans wasn't perfect. The English army was spread very thin. Large numbers of soldiers had recently left the siege. But the people in the city did not realize that the enemy had weakened. They felt abandoned and almost without hope.

When rumors about the maid and her army reached the city, the people's spirits soared—until Joan appeared along the river with a force everyone thought too small to do any good. But Joan scoffed when the Orléans commander, Count Jean Dunois, complained that her force was too small. "I bring you better succor [aid] than has reached you from any soldier or any city," Joan told him when they met outside the city. "It is the succor from the King of Heaven. It comes not from love of me but from God himself."

Joan's army filled rafts and boats with food and supplies. Thanks to a sudden shift in the wind, they were able to sail quickly past the English strongholds and reach the city via the river. The commander's hope was immediately restored, and he persuaded Joan to leave her army and come with him into Orléans.

Joan entered on the evening of April 29, 1429, traveling through the gates around 8 P.M. Dunois wanted her to enter that late to avoid drawing a crowd, but she was mobbed anyway. The people of the city had heard the rumors about her and the voices. They were sure that she was their salvation. They greeted her as they might greet God himself. The mood in Orléans went from despair to triumph overnight—even though Joan had yet to fight a battle.

Plans were made to attack the English. Joan's army

returned without her to the city of Blois, where they could cross the river and march to attack. In the meantime, Joan sent word to the English commanders that they must surrender.

The English reacted with curses. They, too, had heard the rumors about the maid, but they believed she must be a witch. The English commander threatened to burn her messenger. "Let him have me burnt," said Joan, "if he can catch me."

THE ENGLISH HESITATE

While she waited in Orléans for her army to arrive, Joan inspected the city. Deciding to learn more about the English battlements, she went out to see them— not with soldiers but with the people of Orléans: men, women, and children. For some reason, whether they were surprised or perhaps afraid, none of the English soldiers made a move against Joan. She and the people returned in time for services at the city cathedral. She led the whole group not only in prayer but also in tears. She knew the city's freedom was only a few days away.

Joined by more soldiers at Blois, the French army marched toward Orléans. On May 4, Joan went out to meet the army, again accompanied by the common people. Once again, the English mysteriously dared not attack. The French entered the town without an arrow fired against them.

But the English had their own reinforcements on the

The siege of Orléans

way. Joan was anxious and eager to attack before they arrived. Some of her commanders were delaying the attack, which bothered her a great deal. Some were also scheming to act without her.

After dinner on May 4, Joan went to bed to rest. A short while later, she woke with a shout. French blood was flowing, and the voices had told her to fight the English. She dressed in her armor and found a French force retreating from an English battlement on the east side of the city.

Horses reeled, threatening to bolt. Swords and maces clashed frantically in the wild chaos of the fight. The battle might have started out highly organized—with knights on horseback leading soldiers with bows, lances, and swords. But once the fighting began, everything began to whirl. Knights dismounted to fight on foot and raced back and forth rallying groups of soldiers. The English fired hails of arrows, then charged out to meet their foes in hand-to-hand combat. Bowmen fired arrows back and forth. Spiked poles and pikes rammed through the armor of knights and charging foot soldiers. The battle raged in a swirl of blood, dust, and confusion.

The French were losing. They fell back, disorganized. Then Joan arrived. She shouted from her horse that they must not retreat—they must go on the offensive. She wheeled her horse in the direction of the enemy, showing her troops the way. The soldiers regained their courage. Her standard gave them a rallying point as it fluttered over the battle, clearly showing where they must attack. The English were overrun.

When the battle was won, Joan wept at the bloodshed. She said she was sorry to see so many men die without having received confession. She was referring to the English—not the French. She was as worried about the fate of their souls as she was about the fate of her own troops.

The battle had been won the day before the Catholic feast of Ascension, which commemorates Jesus' return to heaven, forty days after Easter. Joan said that there must be no battle on that day.

On Ascension Day, she again sent word to the English, asking them to surrender. The English commander replied with insults. Joan began to weep, asking God to help her. A witness said later that her voices must have returned then, for she suddenly seemed happier and ready for what lay ahead.

Early the next morning, Joan led her forces in an attack on one of the English strongholds. The Frenchmen traveled by boat, bypassing the strongest point of the defenses to strike at a weak spot. But the English realized the French plan and began pulling back to a better position. They gathered together in a large group, which would be more difficult to defeat.

The French plan had been thwarted. As the French began to retreat, the English saw an advantage. They came out from behind their battlements and began to attack. Joan, dressed in her armor and on horseback, took her lance and rushed against them. Her troops rallied to help her, and the English attackers were defeated.

Joan had not been trained as a foot soldier, let alone as a knight. Her lance, ten to twelve feet long and made of wood, was a potent weapon wielded from the back of a horse, but it was heavy and difficult to use. Her suit of armor, most likely made of metal plates and chain mail, weighed as much as fifty-five pounds. Her sword was an old one. But Joan mastered her equipment. She managed not only to inspire her troops but also to fight with them at the head of the battle.

Though they had lost the skirmish, the English still had several strongholds around the city. A large one controlled the bridge across the Loire. This fortification was the most serious threat to the city, and it was the place Joan wanted to attack next.

That night, the French army captains held a council. They told Joan that they did not want to attack the English, fearing themselves to be outnumbered. Since there was now food in the city, they told her, they preferred to wait for the Dauphin to arrive with more troops. At least one historian thinks that this plan was just a trick meant to keep Joan from getting credit for the victory. If so, she didn't fall for it.

"You have been at your counsel and I at mine," she told the commanders, referring to her voices. "My Lord's counsel will be accomplished and will prevail." Then she warned one of her attendants that she would be wounded the next day. "Blood will flow out of my body above my breast," she said.

And so it did. The next day, the French forces began their assault. The English were protected by a great wall and a moat. As they attacked, the French threw ladders into the moat, and men began to climb the wall. But the English were able to hold them off. The attack faltered. The French forces were about to retreat. "Courage!" shouted Joan to her men. "Do not fall back! In a little, the place will yours!"

Joan rode her horse through the chaotic bands of soldiers, shouting and encouraging them. Her flag waved, and light glinted off her armor as the men rallied to her. The French soldiers changed direction, forming attack lines to storm the walls again. "Watch! When you see the wind blow my banner against the bulwark, you shall take it!" she shouted.

Joan rushed down to the moat and slammed a ladder against the wall. As she did, an arrow struck her between her neck and shoulder. Even wounded, she screamed to her men, urging them to scale the ladder.

But the English were not ready to surrender. With Joan wounded, the French attack faltered again. A group of English soldiers came out from behind their walls, lances and swords flashing. Arrows streamed overhead. Joan's men just barely managed to carry her to safety as the English surged toward her, trying to capture her and end the attack.

Lying on the grass, her armor removed, Joan cried out when she saw how deeply the arrow had struck. But once again she heard the voices. Once again she

Joan was wounded in battle, just as the voices had warned her she would be.

became calm and confident. She rose, accepted olive oil and lard—the common treatment for wounds during this era—and returned to Count Dunois, who was thinking about giving up the assault.

Joan told him to wait a while. She went into a vineyard nearby and prayed. When she returned to the battle, she hoisted her flag—and the French soldiers began to rally again. During the confusion, one of her soldiers took her flag. Other soldiers thought she was struggling with him. Some may have believed that the man was the enemy, or that Joan had fallen. The French soldiers charged ahead, hustling first to Joan's rescue and then, when they saw she was unhurt, on to the English positions. Soon they had won a great victory.

The five hundred English soldiers who guarded the fort were either slaughtered or jumped into the river trying to flee and drowned. One of them was the captain of the English, who had called Joan a whore. When she saw that he was dead, she wept for his soul.

By then, the bells of the town were ringing. Orléans had been saved. May 8 would be celebrated as a holy day in the city ever after.

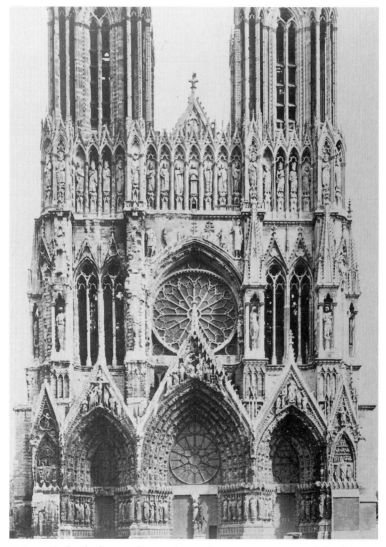

Reims Cathedral was the traditional coronation site of the kings of France.

Chapter SIX

TO REIMS

ORLÉANS HAD BEEN SAVED, BUT JOAN'S WORK was only partly done. The voices had told her to free Orléans *and* have the king crowned at Reims, which was far to the north, in an area controlled by the English. Great armies of the enemy still patrolled the land.

The English had retreated from Orléans, but they had not left France. They had not given up the claim that their young king was heir to the French throne. And the leader of Burgundy was still leading armies against the Dauphin.

Word of Joan's victory at Orléans spread quickly. Many people interpreted the victory as a sign from God, but some saw it as the devil's work. The English, specifically, believed that Joan was a witch, and they

claimed that the French had won only through her en-
chantments. Throughout France, the question of
whether Joan was working for God or the devil was
debated. People's opinions usually depended on
whether they sided with the English or the Dauphin.

One biographer points out that many facts about
Joan were not surprising or out of character during
the Middle Ages. Women had fought before, usually
helping to defend their cities and towns. And many
people had visions that they believed were from God.
There were many good leaders and soldiers, of course,
and certainly many devout Catholics. But Joan com-
bined all these qualities in a unique way. Not only
that, she also proved herself by defeating a powerful
enemy just when the situation seemed bleakest.

Had Joan been a young nobleman, perhaps she
would not have seemed unique. She certainly would
not have been accused of being a witch. But perhaps
she was able to convince the king, in part because she
was so unusual.

Others in the king's circle of friends and advisers—
noblemen and women—had assured him that he was
the true king. Still other noblemen and women had
told him to raise an army and free Orléans. But he
had hesitated until a poor girl from a backward village appeared and spoke.

As a captain, Joan's lack of formal military training
could have hurt her since she didn't know all that a
knight or a captain was normally taught. But her in-

experience also gave her a viewpoint different from other commanders. She might not think that a military situation was hopeless because she judged it by different standards. That attitude could be an asset or a disadvantage, depending on the circumstances.

Joan's uniqueness may have been the reason that so many soldiers followed her into battle. After all, no ordinary woman would lead an army. That fact made it all the more believable that God was speaking through her.

Besides faith in God, Joan's exhortations against the English must have been something the soldiers wanted to hear. Her patriotism was probably just as inspiring as her devotion. And if Joan had no other special powers as a captain, she had one that all great leaders possess: She made other people believe in themselves and their potential. She made the French believe they could win, because God—through Joan— had said they would.

To Be Crowned King

After the victory at Orléans, the Dauphin met Joan with great joy. But his advisers were split over what he should do next. Some wanted him to attack Brittany and other areas to the northwest. Joan wanted him to go to Reims, northeast of Paris, where French kings had been crowned since the tenth century. A coronation there would send a powerful message that the Dauphin was the right and true king.

But Reims was in enemy territory. To get there, the Dauphin would have to fight his way across hundreds of miles, through many enemy cities. The Dauphin decided to continue fighting in the Loire Valley, pursuing the English there—a cautious move that would not overextend his forces.

The next great battle occurred on June 10, 1429, at Jargeau, a town along the Loire not far from Orléans. During the attack, Joan carried her standard up a ladder against the town wall. A rock struck her on the head so hard that it split her helmet. She fell to the ground but immediately rose and rallied her forces. "Friends," she cried, "friends, up, our Lord has condemned the English, in this hour they are ours, be of good heart!"

Inspired by a woman seemingly tougher than they were, all of the French soldiers surged forward. A second ladder joined Joan's, and a third. Soon a multitude of men were swarming over the wall. They seemed to flood the defenders, overwhelming them. By the end of the assault, eleven hundred English soldiers lay dead.

A week later, an even greater battle loomed, this one northwest of Orléans in the area of Patay. The English commanders had gathered their troops together. The French commanders were leery, afraid they were overmatched. Joan was confident. She told her cavalry to make sure they wore their spurs—they would need them to pursue the enemy army when it fled her forces.

Joan's confidence and faith inspired the men in her army to continue fighting despite the odds.

The armies lost each other in the woods and bushes. Finally, a stag ran into one of the English lines, giving their position away. In the battle that followed, two thousand English soldiers were killed, and one of their commanders was captured. The French forces lost only three men. Once again, Joan had prophesied, and then led, a great victory.

It was common at the time to kill prisoners who could not offer ransom—payment to spare their lives. Even though this practice was accepted by armies and leaders, Joan hated it. She favored letting enemy soldiers go free after a battle, if they simply promised not to fight again. After the battle at Patay, she saw one of her men brutally strike a prisoner. She jumped from her horse and cradled the man in her arms until he died.

The victory at Patay was enough to break the English army and its hold on the local countryside. The English retreated northward, while Joan and others urged the king to march north as well. "Sound trumpets and to horse!" Joan shouted to the captains of the army in Orléans on June 24. "It is time to rejoin our noble King Charles and set him on the road to his anointing at Reims!"

But Joan's army and the rout of the English were still not enough to convince all of the Dauphin's court. They debated strategy for several days, arguing that moving north posed many dangers. "All this I know well," Joan said when she was allowed to address the assembly, "but I account it as nothing. By my staff! I shall lead noble King Charles and his company safely, and he shall be anointed in Reims!"

The Dauphin had had trouble raising a large enough army to face the English in the past. But Joan declared that he would no longer have this problem. "We shall find none who can harm us," she told the Dauphin and his counselors. "Indeed, we shall meet with no resistance. I have no fear for lack of men. There will be many to follow me."

Finally convinced, the Dauphin began his long march north from the Loire Valley. Joan's words proved true—momentum in the great war had switched to the Dauphin. Some princes who had opposed him came over to his side. And as his army continued fighting the English, more and more people joined the cause. Partisans, similar to modern-day guerrillas, began to work against the English behind their own lines. They would continue fighting to have a French king for many years.

As the Dauphin's army marched north, one obstacle lay between them and Reims. A large group of English and Burgundian soldiers had occupied the city of Troyes. By the beginning of July, the Dauphin stood at the city gates. And stood. And stood. For the city was large and not to be taken easily. The Dauphin's army was hungry. They did not have siege weapons such as catapults and heavy cannons. Many of his counselors called for retreat.

The coronation of King Charles VII. Joan stands behind him, looking toward heaven.

Once again, though, Joan's enthusiasm and leadership led to victory. Not willing to retreat or wait, she took her standard to the moat that surrounded the city walls. Foot soldiers and others followed. They filled the moat with everything available, from bushes to tables and chairs. Filling the moat would make it easy to scale the city walls. The people inside saw that they would be overrun and quickly surrendered to the Dauphin. Farther north, the leaders of Reims surrendered as well. The Dauphin entered the city on July 16, 1429.

He was crowned king the next day. Joan's standard was given a place of honor at the great cathedral that held the holy ceremony. And among the crowd that witnessed the coronation of Charles VII were two peasants who had traveled nearly as far as the Dauphin and who must have been almost as elated at Joan's great feats: her mother and father.

Joan in Paris

Chapter **SEVEN**

MIRACLES AND HESITATIONS

THE INFANT WAS TINY—BARELY THREE DAYS OLD.
It had not moved since it was born. Its white skin had
turned black—horrible to look at. All who saw the
baby thought for sure it was dead. Yet its mother
clung to the hope that it was somehow still alive, for
the small infant had not been baptized. Without baptism, Catholics believed, a soul would be condemned
to Limbo, a place that was neither heaven nor hell.
The mother refused to let go of the baby, afraid of
dooming it to a horrible eternity. She insisted that it
be baptized—but this was impossible while it showed
no sign of life.

The mother and others in the small town of Lagny
knew Joan of Arc was staying there. Desperate for

some sort of miracle, they brought the infant to her. Moved, Joan went to a statue of the Virgin Mary and began to pray with them.

Suddenly, the infant yawned, stirring to life. Instantly, it was baptized.

Though the baby soon died, its soul had been saved. The mother and the others believed a miracle had surely occurred. And they were equally sure that God had worked the miracle through Joan of Arc, the Maid of Orléans.

FRUSTRATIONS

Joan had come to Lagny in the spring of 1430, following a year of frustrations. After being crowned king, Charles had once more become cautious. In the summer of 1429, Joan had joined an attack on Paris, which was in enemy hands. She said later that her voices had not told her to go. She went only because some noblemen wanted her to fight there.

During the attack, a crossbow bolt had struck her in the thigh. Seriously injured, she insisted on staying as the battle continued. It wasn't until late at night that her soldiers finally managed to drag her away from the fighting.

Joan soon recovered, but the attack on Paris was called off by the king. He made a truce with the Duke of Burgundy, the English king's main ally in France. Charles later realized that the duke had tricked him, signing the truce just to buy time for himself and the

English. The duke was gaining power and was not prepared to recognize Charles as the rightful king.

In the meantime, the English were gathering their forces to fight. They tried to discredit Charles's coronation by criticizing Joan. They made a special issue of the fact that she wore men's clothes, which was against the customs and laws of the time. They also implied that she was a prostitute. This accusation was far from the truth. In those days, it was common for prostitutes to accompany an army as it traveled. Joan had forcefully sent the women away and even broke her sword hitting one of them.

Joan of Arc, sleeping in full armor, receives heavenly guidance.

Many months passed before Charles realized that he had been duped by the duke. By then, the English and Burgundian forces were again on the move. The Duke of Burgundy poured his resources into the war, believing in the end that he would benefit. The English had placed him in charge of Paris and left much of the fighting to him. He took up the attack on cities and territories loyal to Charles.

Shortly after Joan helped baptize the infant at Lagny, the Duke of Burgundy's army began marching toward Compiègne, a city roughly thirty miles north of Paris. Joan was determined to continue the fight and set out with her forces to find the enemy. Before she did, however, she had a premonition of her fate.

Saint Catherine and Saint Margaret appeared to her

Saint Catherine appeared to Joan from the age of thirteen until her death.

STORIES OF THE SAINTS

The saints—Catherine and Margaret—who visited Joan were popular during the Middle Ages. According to legend, Catherine lived in Alexandria, Egypt (part of the Roman Empire), around the end of the third century A.D. When she was eighteen years old, she had a vision, which prompted her to become a Catholic. She confronted the Roman emperor about persecuting Christians. To silence her, he sent her to the empire's most learned men. But she spoke so well that she converted them to Christianity. The emperor then tried to bribe her and, finally, to silence her with torture. In the end, Catherine was beheaded. But because she was so pure, milk—not blood—was said to flow from her veins.

Saint Margaret was said to have lived in the third or fourth century A.D. in Antioch in what is now Turkey. As a young girl, she was thrown out of her house by her father because she had converted to Christianity, which was then against the law. To survive, she became a shepherdess. When she resisted the attempts of a local official to make love to her, the man told the authorities that she was a Christian. She was tortured but would not renounce her religion. Margaret survived many ordeals, including burning. Finally, she was beheaded.

Despite the popularity of these stories, modern historians doubt that either Catherine or Margaret actually lived.

and warned that she would be taken prisoner before Saint John's Day in June. There was no way to avoid capture, they told her. It was God's will. And so she submitted herself to this fate and rode to Compiègne to see what might be done in the meantime.

To ward off enemy attacks, most French castles in the 1400s were fortified with thick stone walls, such as the castle at Beaurevoir, above.

Chapter **EIGHT**

GLORY'S END

JOAN WAS IN CRÉPY WHEN THE NEWS CAME THAT Compiègne, less than twenty miles from her as the crow flies, was besieged. By midnight, she had gathered her troops and set out. She had only three or four hundred soldiers. Many warned her it was too small a force to meet the English and Burgundian troops around the town. But Joan would not be deterred.

She and her troops rode all night. By daybreak on May 23, 1430, her force, untouched by the enemy, reached the city. Around nine o'clock that morning, the Burgundian forces began skirmishing with the town's defenders in a field outside the town. Joan put on her armor and took her horse to join the fight. The two sides met a short distance from the drawbridge outside of the town gate.

The combat was fierce, but neither side could gain an advantage. As evening approached, the French forces began to withdraw. They retreated slowly from the meadow, back toward the bridge. According to Joan's account of the battle, the English forces attempted to ambush her troops, attacking from behind to cut off their approach to the bridge.

As usual, Joan helped protect her men as they retreated into the city. She goaded her horse to stay between her troops and the enemy. The English and Burgundian forces were so close to the city that the drawbridge was raised and the gate closed. Joan and some of her men were left outside. In the roiling battle that followed, she was pulled from her horse and swarmed by the enemy.

A member of the Burgundian forces heard about the battle shortly afterward. He wrote that Joan had stayed behind "as captain and bravest of her troop. And there Fortune allowed her glory at last come to an end and that she bear arms no longer. . . . An archer, a rough man and sour, full of spite because a woman of whom so much had been heard should have overthrown . . . so many valiant men, dragged her to one side by her cloth-of-gold cloak and pulled her from her horse, throwing her flat on the ground."

Joan struggled to get up. Her men, including her brother Pierre, tried desperately to rescue her. It was no use. The enemy overwhelmed them. Joan of Arc, the Maid of Orléans, the savior of France, surrendered to a Burgundian knight and was spirited away.

Joan is interrogated in her prison cell.

Chapter **NINE**

PRISONER

THE **ENGLISH AND BURGUNDIAN ARMIES CELEBRATED** as if they had captured the king himself. The French in Compiègne were more depressed than if the king had been killed. John of Luxembourg, the knight who had taken Joan, had her brought from the battle camp to the castle of Beaulieu. Since John was part of the Burgundian forces, Joan was a prisoner of the Duke of Burgundy, not of the English. But it was the English who truly wanted her.

An eyewitness on the Burgundian side said that, among the English, Joan was the most feared enemy captain. She had won many battles when the odds seemed against her. Her mere appearance on the battlefield could spur her troops onward. She inspired all of France, from peasants to the king. And she wanted to keep fighting until the English were removed from the country.

Her abilities as a commander were not the only reason the English wanted her, however. The English and French were fighting over the right to rule France. The English claimed that a treaty gave their king the right to the throne. He was related to the previous French king and was his rightful heir, they argued. But the French had their own claims and arguments. And all claims were subject to debate—and war.

But if God had said that Charles VII was king, no argument could stand against it—God was viewed as the ultimate judge. If he had truly spoken through Joan, as those who followed her believed, then the French were right. No interpretation of facts or laws, no argument and no war, could overturn God's decision. In fact, to go against God's word would be to commit the gravest of sins.

The idea of a peasant girl leading an army into battle and defeating knights seemed incredible, even impossible. Those of her sex and class never led battles, let alone won them. But Joan gave all the credit to the voices, claiming that God had given the French army victory—she was just God's tool. The French agreed.

The English thought God favored them, rather than the French. So, obviously, they didn't think God would be helping the French win. There had to be another explanation. According to English arguments, Joan could not be speaking or acting for God. The English claimed the opposite had to be true—her victories had to be due to the devil.

The English had been saying that Joan was a witch since the battle at Orléans. They believed that she worked with the devil and possessed special powers because of him. Those powers—and therefore the devil, not God—had caused the English to lose. Since Joan had been captured, they had a chance to prove it—if the English could get her away from the duke's men.

THE KING DOES NOTHING

Charles VII had benefited greatly from Joan of Arc. She had led him to Reims. Without her, he might never have saved his land or gained so much support. But after Joan was captured, he did not try to free her. He did not offer ransom for her return. He did not send an army to rescue her.

Historians have debated the reasons. Charles VII may have feared Joan. He may have listened to advisers who did not like her. He may have thought that God had caused her to be captured. Or he may just have felt too weak to rescue her. Whatever the reason, the result was the same: Charles VII did nothing. Joan remained far behind enemy lines, with little hope of rescue.

She was taken to a castle at Beaulieu, where she tried to escape but was seen and recaptured. Moved to a castle at Beaurevoir, she thought of leaping from the tower where she was held. Her voices commanded her not to, but Joan jumped anyway. One biographer estimates that the tower was sixty feet high. Joan was hurt so badly she could not eat or drink afterward.

"The reason why I jumped from the tower was that I had heard that all the people in Compiègne, even children of seven years, were to be put to fire and sword," she said later. "And I would rather be dead than live on after such a destruction of good people." That was one reason. "The other was that I knew that I was sold to the English, and I thought death would be better than to be in their hands who were my enemies."

Joan had disobeyed the voices and begged them to forgive her. Saint Catherine told her to be of good cheer. Not only would she recover from her wounds, but the people of Compiègne would be saved.

Joan remained at Beaurevoir for many months. She was a prisoner, yet she impressed many of the people who saw her there. A priest who said Mass and heard confessions believed she was very good and devout. The wife of Joan's captor threw herself at his feet, pleading that Joan be kept from the English.

Since leaving Vaucouleurs, Joan had worn men's clothing. At Beaurevoir, she was offered a woman's dress. She refused to wear it, saying that it "was not yet time"—that God had not yet given her permission to take off the clothes of war and return to her existence as a poor countrywoman.

Throughout the spring, summer, and early fall, the English worked to have Joan brought to them. They did not simply want to keep her a prisoner. Nor did they plan to return her to the French in exchange for a ransom. They wanted to have her put on trial by the Church. In that way, the world could be shown that she was working for the devil. Charles VII's claim to be king because of God's will would be shown to be false.

At the time, church leaders played important roles in politics. Bishops and cardinals were very powerful in government, much like modern politicians. The Cardinal of Winchester, Henry Beaufort, was one such leader. Not only was he a church leader, but he was also a great-uncle of the King of England—and very active in politics. Historians believe he worked hard behind the scenes to bring Joan to trial.

The English enlisted Pierre Cauchon, the Bishop of Beauvais, to act on their behalf. They also convinced the local head of the Inquisition—the arm of the Catholic Church charged with prosecuting religious crimes—that Joan should be tried. Together, the two men charged Joan with heresy and similar religious crimes. They claimed she was working with the devil and that she was a witch.

In its simplest form, heresy was to disagree with or go against an important belief of the Church. Church and society were so intertwined in Joan's time that heresy could range from simply thinking that women should be allowed to wear men's clothing to believing that the devil was more important than God. The most severe penalty for heresy was to be burned at the stake.

On behalf of the King of England, Cauchon went to the Duke of Burgundy and offered a ransom of ten thousand francs for Joan. This was as much money, Cauchon said, as would be offered for a king. The English also put economic pressure on the duke. The duke agreed to their terms, and Joan was handed over for trial in November 1430.

She was taken to Rouen in Normandy, an area long under English control and far from any large French force. Church officials nearby were thought to be sympathetic to the English.

A STAGED TRIAL

There were only two judges at Joan's trial. One was Pierre Cauchon, who had been employed to get Joan from the duke. A receipt from the time survives to show that he was directly on the English payroll. The other judge was Jean LeMaitre, the head of the Inquisition at Rouen. He spent as little time as possible at the long trial. He did not interfere with the proceedings and clearly wanted nothing to do with them.

Besides the judges, about sixty church officials worked as court officers. They were called assessors, or sometimes simply judges, though they were not judges but actually consultants to them. Among them

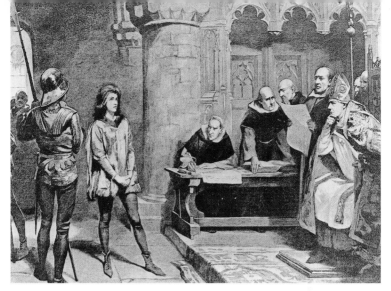

Joan of Arc faces church officials at her trial.

was the Cardinal of Winchester, Henry Beaufort, a powerful influence on the proceedings. Many other assessors were on the English payroll or simply sided with the English. Some wanted revenge on Joan. Others thought they would gain power or money by participating in her trial. Still others were pushed into taking part and were afraid to refuse the position.

The Inquisition court worked very differently than modern courts. The judges and assessors asked all the questions. There was no one we would call a prosecutor, except for the judges and assessors themselves, and no lawyer assigned to defend Joan. The judges also acted as the jury—they decided guilt or innocence.

In short, the English had decided Joan's fate before the trial ever began. They chose the place for the trial and pressured the judges and the court officials. They decided that if heresy could not be proven—if they somehow lost their case—that Joan would be taken back and kept as their prisoner.

Joan defends herself at her trial.

Chapter TEN

ON TRIAL

THE JUDGE LOOMED BEFORE HER. **"HAVE YOU** fasted every day of this Lent?" he asked.

"What has that to do with your trial?" Joan replied calmly. She was standing in the castle at Rouen, an English stronghold and her prison. It was February 1431, many months after she'd been captured and about two years after her incredible journey began.

"Yes, indeed, it belongs to the trial," insisted the judge. He and the others had been questioning her for several days. Their questions were relentless—often asked so quickly that the judges and assessors would interrupt each other. At times the men seemed innocent and even friendly. Then they would turn biting and mocking.

"Yes, certainly," Joan told them. "I have fasted the whole time."

"Have you heard the voice since Saturday?" asked the judge.

"Yes, indeed, many times," said Joan.

"Did you hear it in this hall on Saturday?"

"That has nothing to do with your trial," she told him. Joan knew the judges did not believe the voices came from the saints. They thought she had either made them up or—if they were real—that they came from the devil. They would have her burned if she would not admit it. They might anyway.

"Yes, I heard the voice," Joan said finally.

"What did it say to you?"

"I did not well understand it. I understood nothing that I could tell you until my return to my room."

"And what did it say when you got back to your room?"

"That I should answer you boldly," she said, refusing to be intimidated by the men who mocked her and her beliefs.

TRIAL BY WORDS

Joan had faced swords, arrows, and stones. She had been wounded in battle at least three times. She had seen much blood—her men's, the enemy's, her own. She had wept for the deaths of many men on both sides. She had not broken.

This time, she faced a new onslaught. Gathered

against her were the toughest inquisitors the English force could find. Closely guarded, deprived of her friends and even simple comforts, Joan was questioned and tried for five months. She was kept in chains, without a lawyer or advocate to help plead her case. In fact, anyone who tried to even give her advice risked his own life. One guard sometimes allowed her to stop and pray in the prison chapel as they walked to the trial. He was threatened with jail.

The court sessions were designed to intimidate Joan. Trick questions were common. Joan fended them off and even made jokes at the expense of her questioners. One day, a trial official asked her about the archangel Michael, asking how he appeared.

"I saw no crown upon him," Joan answered. "I know nothing of his garments."

"Was he naked?" asked the man.

"Do you think God has not the wherewith to clothe him?" Joan mocked.

But the Inquisition courts were hardly fun and games. The judges and assessors were extremely intimidating. They could reduce the proudest man or woman to a whimpering fool. Such courts usually followed rules of fairness—but these rules were broken in Joan's case. Those keeping the records included only information that helped the prosecution. Spies pretending to be Joan's allies and friends were sent to wring information from her.

Yet Joan stood firm. Again and again, the questioners

tried to pry words from her that would prove she was
a heretic [nonbeliever]. They wanted her to admit that
she worked with the devil. They wanted her to say
that the saints were more important than the Church,
which she did not say. To make such a claim would
amount to heresy.

Since all the court officers were part of the Church,
Joan might easily have found reason to criticize it.
But she did not. "Will you leave to the determination
of our Holy Mother the Church, all your matters
whether in good or in evil?" demanded one of the inquisitors during a typical session.

"As for the Church, I love her and would wish to
sustain her with all my power for our Christian faith,"
she answered. "And it is not I who should be pre-
vented from going to church and hearing Mass."

"Will you abide by the Church's determination for
your sayings and deeds?"

"I abide by God who sent me, by the Holy Virgin
and all the saints in paradise. And I am of opinion
that it is all one and the same thing, God and the
Church, and that of that one should make no difficulty. Why do you make difficulty over that?"

The questioning continued, with the inquisitors
drawing a line between the Church in heaven and the
Church on earth. Joan told him that she had been
sent to the king of France—her king, not England's—
by God and the Church above. Of the Church on
earth, she would not say anything else.

Joan's faith continued to grow while she was in prison.

"What say you of that women's clothing which is offered you that you may go and hear Mass?" asked the judge.

"As for women's clothing, I shall not put it on until it please God," she replied. "And if it should be that I must be brought even to judgment, I trust in the lords of the Church that they will grant me the mercy of having a woman's shift and a covering for my head. And I would rather die than revoke what God has made me do."

MORE THAN JUST CLOTHES

Historians still debate why Joan wore only men's clothing after leaving Vaucouleurs. The reasons may have ranged from practical to symbolic to religious. For example, the best thing to wear in battle was a suit of armor—which was designed for a man. The leaders of the army always dressed a certain way—doing so made Joan look like the other leaders. Most important, Joan's voices had told her that God wanted her to dress that way.

In medieval times, however, it could be considered a crime or heresy for women to dress in men's clothes. For a woman to pretend to be a man was to go against God's order for the universe. Even people who supported Joan thought that her wearing men's clothing was odd. How people interpreted this behavior—whether they thought she was guilty of a crime or not—depended on whether or not they supported her. Their opinions also depended on whether or not they thought God had ordered her to wear the clothes.

To modern people, the charge that Joan committed a crime by wearing men's clothing seems silly. Modern women wear pants all the time. In fact, many of the clothes men wore during the fifteenth century looked more like modern women's clothes than men's. Men's leggings, for example, looked like tights. Their tunics, or shirts, were often long, extending to the knee like dresses.

Most of all, it's hard for modern people to understand how fashion could be a crime. But the charge against Joan was about much more than clothes. The clothes were said to be part of Joan's heresy—a symbol of her crime. And since everyone knew that Joan had worn men's clothing—she wore them at the trial—the charge was very easy to prove.

The judges and assessors were all leaders of the Roman Catholic Church. They could easily have said that the Church did not want her to wear men's clothes. If Joan refused to put on a dress, then she was disobeying the Church. If she claimed her voices told her not to, then she was acting as if her voices were more important than the Church. That was also heresy.

Even so, Joan said that God wanted her to wear men's clothes. If she had to choose whom to obey, the judges or God, she would choose God.

Joan contemplates her confession.

Chapter ELEVEN

CONDEMNED

JOAN ASKED THAT HER CASE BE TAKEN BEFORE
the Pope. He had examined some other cases, but the
inquisitors refused to allow it. The questioning continued for several more weeks. Joan remained stead-
fast. She carefully guarded information about the
voices and would not tell the judges all that the angels had told her. She refused to take an oath to tell
all, for then she would be bound to reveal it.

The judges ordered a physical examination to see if
Joan was really a virgin. Joan submitted—and was
proven to be so. This fact did not support the judges'
case. In fact, it was evidence against them. According
to the thinking of those days, a virgin could not be a
witch, nor could she have made a pact with the devil.

Virgins were also thought to be extremely virtuous—
the opposite of heretics. But the evidence of Joan's
virginity was not included in the record of the trial.

The questioning continued. The case of heresy came
down to Joan's clothes and her refusal to submit to
the Church. Even on those charges, the judges dis-
torted what she said, sometimes recording the exact
opposite. Still, many of the assessors were impressed
by the prisoner. At times, some of them seemed to
help her in small ways, making sure the secretary
wrote down what she said correctly.

Joan told the assessors that Saint Catherine had
promised to provide her with succor, or assistance.
But Joan seemed unsure whether this promise meant
that she would be freed from prison or that she would
become a martyr—killed, but rewarded with everlast-
ing life in heaven.

Finally, the judges ruled that Joan was guilty. The
next step in the procedure was to allow her to *admit*
that she was guilty—as required by Church law. By
admitting guilt, a person might save his or her soul
from eternal damnation. In some cases, the person
might also escape earthly punishment, or at least have
the punishment reduced. In Joan's case, a confession
might save her from being burned as a heretic.

During this time, around Easter, Joan became very
sick. She thought a carp she had eaten had made her
sick. She may have thought she was poisoned. Weak,
believing she would die, she asked that she be given

the Holy Communion and buried in holy ground. Cauchon refused and continued to press her for a confession that she had been working with the devil.

Though it was common to torture prisoners to get them to admit to crimes, Joan seems not to have been physically tortured. She refused to admit any guilt—and much to the anger of the English, continued to impress many of the assessors and others examining her. They pressed Cauchon for an end to the process—and the ultimate punishment of death.

On Thursday, May 24, 1431, Joan was brought to a cemetery. A stake and a pile of wood lay before her. Cauchon and the others told her that if she did not confess she would be burned at the stake. If she did confess, she would be taken from the English and allowed to do penance in a church prison. She would have to wear women's clothing and let her hair grow as a woman's—an important sign of her obedience. She would stay in prison for the rest of her life—but she would not be put to death, and she would be out of English control.

It was a difficult choice, but prison was better than being burned. What's more, a prisoner in a church prison would be given the Holy Communion, which Joan had been denied. Joan signed a confession, called an *abjuration*. Some questioned at the time whether she fully understood what she was signing. It also seems that there were two different statements—one that Joan signed and one the judges put in the record.

The statement Joan signed was very short. It said only that she would "hold all that the judges and the Church said or pronounced, saying that in all she would obey." The statement meant that she would wear women's clothing as a sign of obedience to the Church and that she would not argue about the voices.

The other document, the one included in the official record, was much longer. According to this statement, Joan admitted that she had lied about receiving visions and messages from God. As soon as Joan signed the abjuration, Cauchon had her sent back to prison—to the English, contradicting what he had promised.

BURN HER

The English were not pleased with the trial. Joan had not been found to be a witch. The rival king had not been discredited. If anything, Joan had won more people to her side. Her abjuration was insufficient, the English said.

It is not exactly clear what happened next. Joan had promised not to wear men's clothes, but within a few days she put them back on. This act was critically important since the clothes were a symbol of her crime. To put on men's clothing was to go against the Church, renouncing the abjuration and penance she had agreed to.

Some said that the English took away her dress and left only men's clothes in her prison cell. Others said that an Englishman tried to rape her. Whatever the reason, by Sunday, May 27, she had put on male clothes, and on Monday she denounced the abjuration. "All that I said and revoked that Thursday, I did only because of fear of the fire," she told the judges.

Joan's words meant she took back the confession. She knew that she would be seen as willfully going against the Church. She could be condemned to be burned.

Cauchon stood in front of her. On Thursday, he said, she had admitted that she had lied about the voices— she had lied when she claimed they were Saint Catherine and Saint Margaret. "I did not mean to do and say so. I did not mean to revoke my apparitions," said Joan. "I have never done anything against God and against the faith."

Cauchon left the room. He had gotten the justification he needed to burn her as a heretic. She had made a confession and then revoked it. A cruel death was the only fitting punishment.

Outside, Cauchon laughed to the English lords and guards. "Farewell, farewell, it is done," he told them.

Joan of Arc is led to her execution.

Chapter TWELVE

THE PYRE

ON THE MORNING OF WEDNESDAY, MAY 30, 1431, eight hundred English soldiers armed with axes and swords lined the old market of Rouen near the church of Saint-Sauveur. The market was the place where fish were sold.

At her prison, Joan climbed into a small wooden cart. She was led through the streets, past the crowds, to a scaffold near a massive pile of wood. Pierre Cauchon was there. So were other Church and English officials. Calmly, Joan stood and listened to Cauchon announce that she was guilty.

"We declare that thou, Joan, commonly called the Maid, art fallen into diverse errors and diverse crimes of schism, idolatry, invocation of devils and numerous others," read Cauchon. "We declare thee relapsed and heretic."

The English were impatient. They wanted her burned quickly. Already they had started the fire. They ignored the official protocol, skipping the formal sentencing after Cauchon had Joan handed over to the civil authorities. She was pulled directly by the soldiers to the pyre.

She had received the Eucharist that morning. Throughout the sermon and proceedings, she praised God and the saints.

"Jesus," she said. "Jesus."

She had no cross. An Englishman made a small one

Citizens and soldiers observe preparations for the burning of Joan of Arc.

of wood and gave it to her. She kissed it, then put it next to her body beneath her clothes. She also asked for a cross from the nearby church so she could see it at the moment of her death. It was brought to her. She held it until she was bound to the stake.

The flames began to climb toward her. Sometimes pyres were arranged so that the victim would die quickly or be overcome by smoke before the flames touched him or her. It was not arranged that way for Joan.

"Jesus," she said again and again. She called on the saints to make a place for her in heaven. The fire raged. It could take a long time for a person to die by burning. It was a painful end—body scorched, lungs choked.

Joan recited her prayers the entire time.

Joan of Arc's death touched many who witnessed it. One soldier believed he saw Joan's soul rise to heaven.

Chapter **THIRTEEN**

GOD'S GRACE

AN ENGLISH SOLDIER IN THE MARKETPLACE
boasted to friends that he would throw wood on the
pyre when Joan was burned. As the flames climbed,
he ran to it. Joan, lashed to the stake above him, was
just about to die. He threw his wood, then fell back in
shock. "I saw with her last breath a dove fly out of
her mouth," he swore to his friends later. He believed
he had seen Joan's soul flying to heaven.

Joan's death touched many of those who witnessed
it, including the English. But it did not affect the war
between the English and the French. Both sides continued to fight, with neither gaining a real advantage.

Within a few years, the Duke of Burgundy changed
sides. Turning his back on the English, he made peace

with Charles VII in 1435. Most historians say that this change turned the tide of war in favor of the French. The English and the French signed a truce in 1444. Peace lasted until 1449, when an English raid and an uprising in Normandy rekindled the war. This time, Charles VII's troops and the local citizens forced out the English soldiers. Rouen was taken by the French that fall.

With Rouen in his hands, the king began investigating what had happened to Joan of Arc. While he knew she had been burned as a heretic, he had never received a full or impartial account of her trial. His investigation showed that the English had controlled the trial and its outcome. And since Joan had helped crown Charles king, labeling her a heretic was a criticism of him as well. He and many others believed Joan had been unjustly tried. Many wanted her name cleared. The Church began to investigate, but the process moved very slowly.

Finally, a new trial was scheduled. In November 1455, Joan's mother—very old at this time—journeyed from her new home in Orléans with her three sons and a large group of citizens. They went to Notre Dame Cathedral in Paris. As a tumultuous mob filled the cathedral, they asked that Joan receive a new trial—and justice.

"Although she did never think, conceive or do anything whatever which set her out of the path of the faith . . . certain enemies . . . had her arraigned," her mother declared in a formal document written to launch the new case. "In a trial perfidious, violent, iniquitous and without shadow of right . . . did they condemn her in a fashion damnable and criminal, and put her to death very cruelly by fire."

And so the second trial of Joan of Arc began. It moved from place to place around France, to make it easier for people to testify. At this trial, Joan's friends were able to speak. The assessors who remained alive were also questioned, as were other witnesses.

On July 7, 1456, the court and a crowd gathered at the cemetery where Joan had signed the abjuration. One of the original documents stating the charges against her was torn up and destroyed. Joan, the church had decided, was not a heretic. The next day, the crowd returned to the marketplace where she had been burned. In a solemn ceremony, another copy of the charges was destroyed. Prayers were said. A cross was put up in her memory.

People all across the country celebrated.

DIFFERING VIEWS

Charles VII reigned until 1461. In the years after Joan's death, he reformed the army and the government, making them more professional and efficient. Many of his changes remained in effect for years and influenced events that followed.

Historians have different views about how good a king he was. They also have different views about how important Joan of Arc was in winning the war against the English. Some say the Duke of Burgundy's decision to change sides was most important. Others say that Joan stirred up a feeling of French patriotism against the English that forever changed the country.

Interpretations of Joan of Arc's story have differed greatly from age to age since her death. Ironically, many of those interpretations ignore her deep religious faith and concentrate on politics, with different political groups using Joan as a symbol of their own beliefs. During and after World War I and World War II, for instance, Joan was celebrated as a patriotic hero by many French people. She was often cited as an example of how to fight and resist invading armies.

Joan's patriotism was also cited in the 1990s by people who wanted to "purify" France by excluding immigrants and Jews from the country. Political rallies were held on her feast day—May 30, the day she was burned—and groups raised money in her name to further their aims of "purity." Her kindness and goodwill toward others was forgotten. In a way, what Joan stood for was twisted for purposes she might have considered evil.

Joan has been studied by many feminist scholars, especially since the 1960s and 1970s. Their interpretations of her story vary as well. Many scholars use Joan as an example of how women have been punished for doing things that men are allowed or expected to do, such as fighting in battle or acting as a leader. Other scholars use Joan's life as an illustration of how attitudes toward witchcraft and women have changed over time.

Whatever we may think of these ideas, we should remember that Joan herself was not a feminist. She did not fight for equal rights for women. She did not try to change the roles of men and women in society. From everything she and others said and wrote, it seems clear that Joan believed God told her to drive the English out and to crown the Dauphin king. That alone was her goal.

Even the Catholic Church's attitude toward Joan has changed over the years. At her second trial, the Church found that Joan was not a heretic—but went no further. Some Church leaders still believed she should have obeyed the earthly Church. Others did not believe that the voices she heard were really the saints. The Church did not celebrate Joan for her accomplishments, and it did not say she was a model for others.

Over a long period of centuries, however, some of those feelings changed. In 1920, after World War I had left much of France in ruins, the Catholic Church declared Joan a saint. This decision helped boost morale in the war-torn country. The young woman who had been put to death by the Church was venerated not as a martyr, but as a virgin.

Many books have been written about Joan of Arc, also with different interpretations. The records of her two trials have been preserved and can be read in English translations. Of course, readers reviewing those records must remember that they were written with particular aims in mind: The English wanted to convince everyone that Joan was evil. The French wanted to convince everyone that she was good. The records are also more concerned with her trials than with her life.

WHAT DID SHE HEAR?

The issue of Joan's voices—whether or not they were truly angels—was not addressed in the verdict at the second trial. The question of whether Joan was divinely inspired was left open—as it still is for many people.

One of the assessors at the first trial declared that Joan's voices were not sent from God but were the result of "human aspirations." In other words, he believed that Joan had either lied or deluded herself about hearing them. Many modern people might agree. In our society, someone who claims to hear voices might be diagnosed with a mental disorder called schizophrenia.

Whatever the interpretation of her life, it would be difficult to argue that Joan was not one of the most remarkable young women—indeed one of the most remarkable human beings—of all time. Her courage and devotion to her beliefs were so great that she stood up to armies and a nation and inspired a king and country to follow her.

"Do you know if you are in God's grace?" demanded one interrogator at the height of her rigged trial.

"If I am not, may God bring me to it," she replied. "If I am, may God keep me in it."

SOURCES

21 William Trask, *Joan of Arc, in Her Own Words* (New York: Turtle Point, 1996), 11.
33 Jules Michelet, *Joan of Arc*, trans. Albert Guérard (Ann Arbor: University of Michigan Press, 1957), 19.
34 Régine Pernoud, *Joan of Arc, by Herself and Her Witnesses*, trans. Edward Hyams (New York: Dorset Press, 1964), 56.
35 Pernoud, 58.
36 Ibid., 98.
43 Ibid., 81–82.
44 Michelet, 28.
48 Pernoud, 90.
48 Ibid.
49 Trask, 37.
49 Ibid., 50.
56 Pernoud, 114.
58 Trask, 46.
59 Ibid., 51.
59 Ibid., 51.
70 Pernoud, 151.
76 Trask, 87–88.
76 Pernoud, 156.
82 *The Trial of Joan of Arc*. (Evesham, Great Britain: Arthur James Ltd., 1996), 60–61.
83 Trask, 105.
84–85 Pernoud, 173–174.
85 Ibid., 174.
92 Ibid., 214.
93 Ibid., 222.
93 Ibid.
93 Ibid., 223.
96 Ibid., 230.
99 Ibid., 233
101 Ibid., 265.
104 Georges Duby, *France in the Middle Ages, 987–1460*, trans. Juliet Vale (Cambridge, Mass.: Blackwell, 1991), 296.
105 Pernoud, 183.

BIBLIOGRAPHY

Barrett, W. P., ed. and trans. *The Trial of Jeanne D'Arc.* New York: Gotham House, 1932.

Duby, Georges. *France in the Middle Ages, 987–1460.* Translated by Juliet Vale. Cambridge, Mass.: Blackwell, 1991.

Fowler, Kenneth. *The Age of Plantagenet and Valois.* New York: Exeter Books distributed by Bookthrift, 1967.

France, Anatole. *The Life of Joan of Arc.* Translated by Winifred Stephens. New York: John Lane, 1909.

Gies, Frances. *Joan of Arc: The Legend and the Reality.* New York: Harper & Row, 1981.

Goubert, Pierre. *The Course of French History.* Translated by Maarten Ultee. New York: Franklin Watts, 1988.

Holmes, George. *The Norton Library History of England: The Later Middle Ages.* New York: W. W. Norton & Company, 1962.

Lightbody, Charles Wayland. *The Judgments of Joan.* Cambridge, Mass.: Harvard University Press, 1961.

Michelet, Jules. *Joan of Arc.* Translated by Albert Guérard. Ann Arbor: University of Michigan Press, 1957.

Pernoud, Régine. *Joan of Arc, by Herself and Her Witnesses.* Translated by Edward Hyams. New York: Dorset Press, 1964.

Trask, William, comp. and ed. *Joan of Arc, in Her Own Words.* New York: Turtle Point, 1996.

The Trial of Joan of Arc. Evesham, Great Britain: Arthur James Ltd., 1996.

Tuchman, Barbara W. *A Distant Mirror.* New York: Alfred A. Knopf, 1978.

Wheeler, Bonnie, and Charles T. Wood, eds. *Fresh Verdicts on Joan of Arc.* New York: Garland, 1996.

FOR FURTHER READING

Banfield, Susan, ed. *Joan of Arc*. New York: Chelsea House, 1987.

Garden, Nancy. *Dove and Sword: A Novel of Joan of Arc*. New York: Farrar Straus & Giroux, 1995.

Morpurgo, Michael. *Joan of Arc: Of Domrémy*. New York: Harcourt Brace, 1999.

Shaw, George Bernard. *Saint Joan: A Chronicle Play*. New York: Viking Press, 1989.

Twain, Mark. *Personal Recollections of Joan of Arc*. New York: Harper & Brothers, 1896.

INDEX

OTHER TITLES FROM LERNER AND A&E®:

Arthur Ashe
Bill Gates
Bruce Lee
Chief Crazy Horse
Christopher Reeve
George Lucas
Gloria Estefan
Jacques Cousteau
Jesse Owens
Jesse Ventura
John Glenn
Legends of Dracula

Louisa May Alcott
Madeleine Albright
Maya Angelou
Mother Teresa
Nelson Mandela
Princess Diana
Queen Cleopatra
Rosie O'Donnell
Wilma Rudolph
Women in Space
Women of the Wild West

ABOUT THE AUTHOR

Jeremy Roberts is the pen name of Jim DeFelice. He often uses this name when he writes for young readers, which he tries to do as much as he can. Besides this biography, his recent nonfiction books include works on skydiving and rock climbing. He has written several installments in the Eerie, Indiana series and quite a few horror tales. His adult books include a historical trilogy and techno-thrillers. He lives with his wife and son in a haunted farmhouse in upstate New York.

PHOTO ACKNOWLEDGMENTS

The images in this book are used with the permission of: Stock Montage, Inc., pp. 2, 12, 33, 35, 60; Archive Photos, pp. 6, 16, 21, 80, 98; Corbis/Bettmann, pp. 9, 15, 22, 37, 45, 50, 57, 68, 79; Corbis/Gianni Dagli Orti, p. 10; Hulton-Getty Collection/Liaison Agency, Inc., p. 40; Erich Lessing/Art Resource, pp. 25, 39, 72; The Art Archive, p. 27; North Wind Picture Archives, pp. 30, 88, 96; Air France Photo, p. 52; Giraudon/Art Resource, N.Y., pp. 62, 65, 94; St. Catherine (fresco) by Fra. Bartolomeo (1472–1517), San Marco, Florence, Italy/Bridgeman Art Library, p. 66; Tate Gallery, London/Art Resource, N.Y., p. 85; Robert Kalman/courtesy of the author, p. 112.

Front cover, back cover: Stock Montage, Inc.